SUCCEEDING WITH WHAT YOU HAVE

Charles Schwab

**Executive
Books**

Life-Changing Classics, Volume X

SUCCEEDING WITH WHAT YOU HAVE
Charles Schwab

Published by
Executive Books
206 West Allen Street
Mechanicsburg, PA 17055
717-766-9499   800-233-2665
Fax: 717-766-6565
www.ExecutiveBooks.com

ISBN: 1-933715-00-6

Cover Design and Interior Layout
by Gregory A. Dixon

Printed in the United States of America

TABLE OF CONTENTS

SUCCEEDING WITH WHAY YOU HAVE
By Charles Schwab

Introduction By Andrew Carnegie

When Charlie Schwab first went to work for me he had no ability as far as surface appearances went, other than that possessed by any other day laborer. But Charlie had an unbeatable mental attitude and a disarming personality that enabled him to win friends among all classes of men.

He also had a natural willingness to do more than he was paid for. This quality was so pronounced in him that he actually *went out of his way to get into the way of work*. He not only went the extra mile, but he added two or three extra miles, and went with a smile upon his face and the right attitude in his heart.

He also went in a hurry and *came back for more* when he had finished any task assigned to him. He took hold on a hard job as eagerly as a hungry man takes on food when it is set before him.

Now, what can one do with a man like that, except to give him plenty of rein and let him go as fast as he pleases? That sort of mental attitude inspires confidence. It also attracts opportunities that would run away from the man who carries a frown on his face and a grouch in his heart.

I tell you frankly that there is no way to hold back a man with that sort of mental attitude. He writes his own price tag *and gets it willingly.* If one employer is shortsighted enough to withhold recognition of such a man, through adequate compensation, some wiser employer will soon discover him and give him a better job. The law of supply and demand, therefore, steps in and forces the proper reward for such a man. The employer has very little to do about such circumstances. *The initiative is entirely in the hands of the employee.*

Word has reached my ears, many times, that Charlie Swab got a favorable "break" because old man Carnegie took a fancy to him and pushed him up front ahead of all the others.

The truth is that Charlie pushed himself up front. All I had to do in the matter was to *keep out of his way and let him go*. Any favorable "break" that he received he created for himself, through his own initiative.

Biography of
Charles M. Schwab

Born in Williamsport, Pennsylvania on February 18, 1862, Schwab grew up in Loretto, Pennsylvania and attended St. Francis College but left in two years to pursue employment opportunities in Pittsburgh. His first job was as a stake driver for Andrew Carnegie's steelworks prior to becoming the president of Carnegie Steel in 1897. Swab also became the first president of U.S. Steel Corporation after he negotiated the buyout of Carnegie Steel in 1901. After resigning from U.S. Steel in 1903, he joined Bethlehem Steel and made it the second-largest steel company in the world. Without any type of organized union, Schwab had proven to be an expert at motivating his men to continually increase productivity through profit sharing incentives and other means.

Schwab was called a motivator of men at Bethlehem Steel. In business, his basic philosophy was to win big or lose big. In reference to an extremely risky venture he took at Bethlehem Steel, he told his secretary, "if we are going to bust, we will go bust big."

In addition to building the Hotel Bethlehem, Schwab was also instrumental in building Bethlehem, Pennsylvania as we know it today by uniting Bethlehem, South Bethlehem, and Northampton Heights into one city. A music lover, Schwab was a big supporter of the Lehigh Valley Orchestra and the Bach Choir in Bethlehem. Charles Schwab brought an enormous amount of wealth and productivity to Bethlehem, PA and could be credited for virtually building the town from the ground up.

In 1929, the stock market crash put a dent in the remainder of Schwab's fortune and he eventually lost "Riverside" and spent his final years in a small apartment. Schwab died bankrupt in London, England on October 18, 1939 and was buried in Loretto. If Schwab would have lived just a few more years, he would have collected millions from his holdings in Bethlehem Steel due to the flood of orders

Bethlehem Steel received for World War II material.

Schwab portrayed a deep appreciation for the common, dedicated working man and he believed in giving the power to succeed to any employer who was willing to pay the price. Schwab pointed out that he motivated his workers by "appeal[ing] to the American spirit of conquest in my men, the spirit of doing things better than anyone has ever done them before."

"In that time it has been my good fortune to watch most of the present leaders rise from the ranks, ascend step by step to places of power," Schwab proclaimed. "These men, I am convinced, are not natural prodigies. They won out by using normal brains to think beyond their manifest daily duty."

1

THINKING BEYOND YOUR JOB

WHEN old Captain Bill Jones, perhaps the greatest leader of men the steel business has ever known, had charge of the Braddock plant for Mr. Carnegie, a call came for a specially capable young man to handle an important piece of engineering at Scotia.

Captain Bill knew men. He picked high-grade assistants with marvelous surety.

"Which one of your draftsmen shall we send up to Scotia?" he asked a superintendent.

"Why, any of them will fill the bill, Captain."

"But there must be one more capable than the others," commented Captain Bill; "who is he?"

"I don't know," and the superintendent shook his head; "they are all bright, hustling youngsters."

Captain Bill stood in thought as his keen eyes ran down the red lines of furnaces. At last he said, "Tell every man to stick on the job until seven o'clock. I'll pick out Scotia's chief for you."

The order was a surprise. It was the slack season, when the draftsmen were not pressed to get through their work in regular hours. But they all kept on cheerfully.

As seven o'clock drew near Captain Bill noticed that the men kept looking up to see how much more time they had to put in. All save one! Over in the corner a young man was so absorbed that he seemed to have forgotten there was a clock in the room. When the hour finally came the others hustled for their coats and hats. This chap was still bending over his desk. He was the man whom Captain Bill sent up to Scotia. One hardly needs to add that later he became a most valued engineer, a high-salaried man.

For thirty-six years I have been moving among workingmen in what is now the biggest branch of American industry, the steel business. In that time it has been my good fortune to watch most of the present leaders rise from the ranks, ascend step by step to places of power. **These men, I am convinced, are not natural prodigies. They won out by using normal brains to think beyond their manifest daily duty.**

American industry is spilling over with men who started life even with the leaders, with brains just as big, with hands quite as capable. And yet one man emerges from the mass, rises sheer above his fellows; and the rest remain.

The men who miss success have two general alibis: "I'm not a genius" is one; the other, "There aren't the opportunities today there used to be."

Neither excuse holds. The first is beside the point; the second is altogether wrong.

The thing that most people call "genius" I do not believe in. That is, I am sure that few successful men are so-called "natural geniuses."

There is not a man in power at our Bethlehem steel works today who did not begin at the bottom and work his way up, round by round, simply by using his head and his hands a little more freely and a little more effectively than the men beside him. Eugene Grace, president of Bethlehem, worked in the yard when I first knew him. Mr. Snyder was a stenographer, Mr. Mathews a draftsman. **The fifteen men in direct charge of the plants were selected not because of some startling stroke of genius but because, day in and day out, they were doing little unusual things—thinking beyond their jobs.**

When I took over the Bethlehem works I decided to train up its managers as Mr. Carnegie trained his "boys." So I watched the men who were already there, and picked out a dozen. This selection took months. Then I set out to build an organization in which we should be bound together in harmony and kindly cooperation. I encouraged my managers to study iron and steel, markets and men. I gave them all small salaries, but instituted a system whereby each man would share directly in the profits for which he himself was responsible. Every one of those boys "came through." They are wealthy men today; all are directors of the company, some are directors of the corporation.

Most talk about "super-geniuses" is nonsense. I have found that when "stars" drop out, successors are usually at hand to fill their places, and the successors are merely men who have learned by application and self-discipline to get full production from an average, normal brain.

The inventor, the man with a unique, specialized talent, is the only real super-genius. But he is so rare that he needs no consideration here.

I have always felt that the surest way to qualify for the job just ahead is to work a little harder than any one else on the job one is holding down. One of the most successful men I have known never carried a watch until he began to earn ten thousand dollars a year. Before that he had managed with a nickel alarm clock in his bedroom, which he never forgot to wind. Young men may enjoy dropping their work at five or six o'clock and slipping into a dress suit for an evening of pleasure; but the habit has certain drawbacks. I happen to know several able-bodied gentlemen who got it so completely that now they are spending all their time, days as well as evenings, in dress suits, serving food in fashionable restaurants to men who did not get the dress-suit habit until some-what later in life.

Recently we have heard much about invest-ments. **To my mind, the best investment a young man starting out in business can pos-sibly make is to give all his time, all his ener-gies, to work—just plain, hard work.** After a man's position is assured, he can indulge in pleasure if he wishes. He will have lost nothing by waiting—and gained much. He will have made money enough really to afford to spend some, and he will know that he has done his duty by himself and by the world.

The man who has done his best has done everything. The man who has done less than his best has done nothing.

Nothing is more fatal to success than taking one's job as a matter of course. If more persons would get so enthused over their day's work that some one would have to remind them to go out to lunch there would be more happiness in the world and less indiges-tion. If you must be a glutton, be a glutton for work. A trained ear can do tremendous busi-ness in the obstruction line. Sometimes it lis-tens so intently for the toot of the quitting whistle that it quite loses the sense of spoken orders.

I have yet to hear an instance where misfortune hit a man because he worked overtime. I know lots of instances where it hit men who did not. Misfortune has many cloaks. Much more serious than physical injury is the slow, relentless blight that brings standstill, lack of advancement, final failure.

The man who fails to give fair service during the hours for which he is paid is dishonest. The man who is not willing to give more than this is foolish.

In the modern business world "pull" is losing its power. "Soft snaps" have been sponged off the slate. In most big companies a thousand stockholders stand guard over the cashier's window, where formerly there were ten. The president's son starts at scratch. Achievement is the only test. The fellow who does the most is going to get the most pay, provided he shows equal intelligence.

Captains of industry are not hunting money. America is heavy with it. They are seeking brains—specialized brains—and faithful, loyal service. Brains are needed to carry out the plans of those who furnish the capital.

The man who attracts attention is the man who is thinking all the time, and expressing himself in little ways. It is not the man who tries to dazzle his employer by doing the theatrical, the spectacular. The man who attempts this is bound to fail.

2

HOW MEN ARE APPRAISED

WHEN I took charge of the Carnegie works at Homestead there was a young chap employed there as water boy. A little later he became a clerk. I had a habit of going over the works at unusual hours, to see how everything was moving. I noticed that no matter what time I came around I would find the former water boy hard at work. I never learned when he slept.

Now, there seemed to be nothing remarkable about this fellow except his industry. The only way in which he attracted attention was by working longer hours and getting better results than any one else. It was not long before we needed an assistant superintendent. The ex-water boy got the job. When we established our great armor plate department there was not the slightest difference of opinion among the partners as to who should be manager. It was the youth with the penchant for overtime service.

Today that ex-water boy, Alva C. Dinkey, is head of a great steel company, and very wealthy. **His rise was predicated on his willingness to work as long as there was any work to be done.**

If a young man entering industry were to ask me for advice, I would say: Don't be afraid of imperiling your health by giving a few extra hours to the company that pays your salary! Don't be .reluctant about putting on overalls! Bare hands grip success better than kid gloves. **Be thorough in all things, no matter how small or distasteful! The man who counts his hours and kicks about his salary is a self-elected failure.**

It may be in seemingly unimportant things that a man expresses his passion for perfection, yet they will count heavily in the long run. When you go into your customary barber shop, you will wait for the man who gives you a little better shave, a little trimmer hair-cut. Business leaders are looking for the same things in their offices that you look for in the barber shop.

The real test of business greatness is in

giving opportunity to others. Many business men fail in this because they are thinking only of personal glory.

Several years ago I was in conference with a New York banker when a news-boy entered the room to deliver a paper. After the boy had left the banker said to me:

"For two years that boy has been bringing me papers every week day. He comes exactly at the time I told him to come, three o'clock. He sells me a paper for just one cent, and neither asks nor expects more. Now a boy who will attend to his business in that fashion has got the right kind of stuff in him. **He doesn't know it yet, but I'm going to put him in my bank, and you may be sure he will be heard from."**

Andrew Carnegie first attracted attention by using his head to think with. It was when he was a telegraph operator on the Pennsylvania Railroad under Colonel Thomas A. Scott. One morning a series of wrecks tangled up the line. Colonel Scott was absent and young Carnegie could not locate him. Things looked bad.

Right then Carnegie disregarded one of the road's strictest rules and sent out a dozen telegrams signed with Colonel Scott's name, giving orders that would clear the blockade.

"Young man," said the superintendent a few hours later, "do you realize that you have broken this company's rules?" ·

"Well, Mr. Scott, aren't your tracks clear and your trains running?" asked the young telegrapher.

Colonel Scott's punishment was to make Carnegie his private secretary. A few years later, when the colonel retired from office, he was succeeded by the former telegrapher, then only twenty-eight years old.

There is a young man in Bethlehem whom I expect to move up. This is the reason: Last winter there was an agitation at Washington which, if successful, would have smashed American shipping and wounded American business. We wanted to lay the matter before the President in its real significance. While we were pondering over ways to accomplish this we got a message from the young man I have mentioned, saying he had seen the President, that the President understood the situation and had come to agree with us.

I wired for this young man to come on to Bethlehem. I wanted to see him. He had initiative; he had been thinking; he had arranged an interview with the President unprompted. In short, he was just the type of man that gladdens the heart of every employer.

Not long ago a man was promoted in our works. "How did you happen to advance this fellow?" I asked his boss.

"Well," he explained, "I noticed that when the day shift went off duty and the night shift came on, this man stayed on the job until he had talked over the day's problems with his successor. That's why!"

I used to have a school friend in Philadelphia who had always impressed me as a forward-looking chap. So I was mightily surprised when he went into his father's business. It seemed to me like a blind-alley choice.

To my surprise, this fellow made an astonishing success. When I met him, several years later, I asked how he had done it.

"If I wanted to make any dent I had to do something different. I pondered ways and means. All I did was climb out of the rut into which other manufacturers had slumped."

A man will succeed in anything about which he has real enthusiasm, in which he is

genuinely interested, provided that he will take more thought about his job than the men working with him. The fellow who sits still and does what he is told will never be told to do big things.

Jimmie Ward, one of our vice-presidents, used to be a stenographer. But he kept doing things out of his regular line of duty. He reminded me of appointments, and suggested little things that helped me get through my work. He was thinking beyond his job, so I gave him a better one. And he has gone up and up.

3

SEIZING YOUR OPPORTUNITIES

EUGENE GRACE is a striking example of what may be accomplished by the man with his eyes fixed further than his pay envelope. Grace's ability to outthink his job, coupled with his sterling integrity, lifted him to the presidency of our corporation. Eight years ago he was switching engines in the yards at Bethlehem. Last year he earned more than a million dollars, and I predict that before long he will be perhaps the biggest man in industrial America.

Even in the humble job of switching engines Grace made himself felt—there is no job too commonplace to express the individuality of an uncommon man. So he was put to operating an electric crane. Then he passed to the open hearth department, at fifteen dollars a week. I watched the fellow: I saw that he was seething with the stuff of which big men are built. He was not strong physically, but that body housed a dynamo of enthusiasm.

He was made yard foreman, then yard superintendent. When we wanted to reorganize the Juragua iron mines in Cuba, Grace got the job. His success was so solid that on his return he was made assistant superintendent to the general manager who had charge of building the twenty-million-dollar Saucon plant at South Bethlehem. Soon he became general superintendent and, only a year later, general manager.

It is a pleasure to do business with Grace. His splendid enthusiasm goes hand in hand with absolute integrity. If he makes a statement you can bet a million on it. You know he is right. This integrity has gone far toward winning him the position he holds today.

Integrity, incidentally, is one of the mightiest factors in salesmanship. If you have a reputation for stating facts exactly, for never attempting to gain momentary advantage through exaggeration, you possess the basis of all successful salesmanship.

Next to integrity comes personality— that indefinable charm that gives to men what perfume gives to flowers. Many of us think of salesmen as people traveling around with sample kits. Instead, we are all salesmen, every day of our lives. We are selling our ideas, our plans, our energies, our enthusiasm, to those with whom we come in contact. Thus, the man of genial presence is bound to accomplish much more, under similar conditions, than the man without it. **If you have personality, cherish it; if you have not, cultivate it. For personality *can* be cultivated, although the task is not easy.**

Nothing is so plentiful in America as opportunity. There are more jobs for forceful men than there are forceful men to fill them. Whenever the question comes up of buying new works we never consider whether we can make the works pay. That is a foregone conclusion if we can get the right man to manage them.

All successful employers of labor are stalking men who will do the unusual, men who think, men who attract attention by performing more than is expected of them. These men have no difficulty in making their worth felt. They stand out above their fellows until their superiors cannot fail to see them.

When A. D. Mixsell, one of our vice-presidents, died a few months ago, every one knew instinctively that his place would be taken by a man named Lewis, an assistant in the auditing department, making, perhaps, two hundred dollars a month. Both Mr. Grace and I picked him out before either had consulted the other. He simply stood out head and shoulders above every one else.

It is a grave mistake to think that all the great American fortunes have been made; that all the country's resources have been developed. **Men make opportunity. Every great industrial achievement has been the result of individual effort—the practical development of a dream in the mind of an individual.**

I know a young New York fellow who has built himself a big business. He used to be a poorly paid clerk in a department store.

One rainy day, when customers were few, the clerks had gathered in a bunch to discuss baseball. A woman came into the store wet and disheveled. The baseball fans did not disband; but this young fellow stepped out of the circle and walked over to the woman. "What can I show you, madam?" he asked, smiling. She told him. He got the article promptly, laid it out before her, and explained its merits courteously and intelligently. In short, he treated the woman just as his employer would have treated her under similar circumstances. When the woman left she asked for his card.

Later the firm received a letter from a woman ordering complete furnishings for a great estate in Scotland. "I want one of your men, Mr. ——," she wrote, "to supervise the furnishing, personally." **The name she mentioned was that of the clerk who had been courteous that rainy day.**

"But, madam," said the head of the firm, a few days later, "this man is our youngest and most inexperienced clerk. Now, hadn't we better send Mr. ——?"

"I want this young man, and no other," broke in the woman.

Large orders impose their own conditions. So our courteous young clerk was sent across the Atlantic to direct the furnishing of a great Scotch palace.

His customer that rainy day had been Mrs. Andrew Carnegie.

The estate was Skibo Castle.

4

THE COLLEGE MAN IN BUSINESS

THE relation of higher education to industry always has interested me. Several years ago I spoke to a little group of New York boys from the East Side on the subject of business success. These youngsters were spending their evenings in hard study after working all day for a living, a splendid indication that they had the right stuff in them.

I told these boys that if they kept to their course they stood as good a chance of success as any boys in the world, a better chance, in fact, than many boys entering college at their age instead of stepping out into the world of practical affairs. **"The higher education for which these boys were giving up three or four of their best years," I said, "holds no advantage of itself in the coming business battle. It will be valueless industrially unless it is accompanied by a capacity for plain,**

hard work, for concentration, for clear thinking. These qualities are not learned in textbooks."

To my utter surprise, the newspapers the next day quoted me as being opposed to a college education, indeed, to education in any form. They declared that I despised learning and believed the time spent in getting it was wasted. This false impression has had a long life. Even today it crops up occasionally.

I am not against a college education. I have never been. Whatever may have been true in the past, there is no doubt that today industrial conditions favor the college man. Old crudities are disappearing; science is dethroning chance. Business is conducted on so vast a scale that the broadening effects of higher education, gained through proper application, write a large figure.

But the college man who thinks that his greater learning gives him the privilege of working less hard than the man without such an education is going to wake up in disaster. I regret that some college men enter industry with an inflated notion of their own value. They want to capitalize at once their education, and the time they spent getting it. They feel it is unfair to begin at the bottom, on the same basis with a boy of seventeen or eighteen who has never been to college.

A college man, entering industry, is worth no more to his employer than a common-school or high-school boy, unless he happens to be taking up some position in which higher education is directly applied. Even then he has to adjust himself. Neither knowledge of the classics nor mathematical proficiency can be converted overnight into a marketable commodity.

Higher education has its chance later, when the college boy has mastered all the minor details of the business. Then, if he went to college with serious purpose, and studied hard and systematically, he has the advantage of a thoroughly trained mind to tackle larger problems, a mind which should be broader and more flexible because of its greater powers of imagination and logical reasoning.

Real success is won only by hard, honest, persistent toil. Unless a young man gets accustomed to that in school he is going to have a very hard time getting accustomed to

it outside. The chap who goes to college only because it suits his parents to send him, and who drifts dreamily through his classes, gets a disagreeable jolt when he lands a job outside with a salary attached to it.

Furthermore, if the college man thinks that his education gives him a higher social status, he is riding for a fall. Some college men, too— not the average ones, fortunately—have a pride in their mental attainments that is almost arrogance. Employers find it difficult to control, guide and train such men. Their spirit of superiority bars the path of progress.

Most college men are free from this false pride. But occasionally employers come in contact with one who has it, and judge all college men by him. In business we buy by sample, and sometimes the wrong sort of sample from an institution of higher learning makes an employer feel as Robert Hall felt when he wrote of Kippis that **"He might be a very clever man by nature, for aught I know, but he laid so many books on top of his head that his brains could not move."**

While I have no sympathy with this occasional prejudice against college men, yet I have found frequently that the very fact of having been denied a higher education works in favor of the common-school boy. He has to labor after hours for his education; nights and holidays he has hammered at the forge of ambition. Success is built on such habits. College men are likely to think their evenings are meant for music, society, the theater, rather than for study that will add to their business knowledge.

For some college men it is a hard descent from the heights of theory to the plains of everyday facts and common sense. **Sometimes years of book learning come to grief before a problem that is disposed of out of hand by men whose wits have been ground to an edge by practical everyday experience.**

Thomas A. Edison, who never saw the inside of a college as a student, once had in his laboratory a man fresh from one of our great universities, where he had been graduated at the head of his class. Soon this young Bachelor of Arts met much that upset his pet theories. But he would not readjust these theories. When things were done contrary to rules laid down in the books, he looked on with indulgence.

One day Mr. Edison unscrewed from its

socket an incandescent electric light bulb. "Find the cubic contents of this!" he said to the college graduate.

To work out the problem by mathematical rote was about as difficult as squaring the circle. But the college student went at it boldly. Reams of paper were figured and disfigured by his energetic pencil during the next few days. Finally he brought to Mr. Edison the result of his calculations. "You're at least ten per cent out of the way," said the inventor. The graduate, sublimely confident, disputed this.

"All right," said Edison calmly. "Let's find out."

The graduate took out his pencil, ready for another siege at mathematics; but the inventor quietly picked up a small hammer and knocked the tip off the blown end of the bulb. Then he filled the bulb with water, weighed it, and in about a minute had arrived absolutely at the result. It showed that the complex mathematical calculations of the college man were at least ten per cent out of the way.

Fortunately, the lesson went home, and afterward the star student became an excellent practical electrician.

5

WHAT YOUR EMPLOYER EXPECTS

BETHLEHEM'S biggest asset is not its rolling mill plants, its gun shops, its armor works, its rail mills; it is the men who make up its enthusiastic organization. For more than thirty years I have been superintending the manufacture of steel, and I can say that my men at Bethlehem are the most energetic, competent and lovable young men with whom I have ever worked.

To no small extent the success of Bethlehem has been built up by our profit-sharing system. But coupled with this individual incentive to extra effort is a corps loyalty, a friendly rivalry, without which no great business can reach the maximum of production.

I love to appeal to the American spirit of conquest in my men, the spirit of doing things better than any one has ever done them before.

There is nothing to which men respond more quickly.

Once when I was with Mr. Carnegie I had a mill manager who was finely educated, thoroughly capable and master of every detail of the business. But he seemed unable to inspire his men to do their best.

"How is it that a man as able as you," I asked him one day, "cannot make this mill turn out what it should?"

"I don't know," he replied; "I have coaxed the men; I have pushed them; I have sworn at them. I have done everything in my power. Yet they will not produce."

It was near the end of the day; in a few minutes the night force would come on duty. I turned to a workman who was standing beside one of the red-mouthed furnaces and asked him for a piece of chalk.

"How many heats has your shift made today?" I queried.

"Six," he replied.

I chalked a big "6" on the floor, and then passed along without another word. When the night shift came in they saw the "6," and asked about it.

"The big boss was in here today," said the day men. "He asked us how many heats we had made, and we told him six. He chalked it down."

The next morning I passed through the same mill. I saw that the "6" had been rubbed out and a big "7" written instead. The night shift had announced itself. That night I went back. The "7" had been erased, and a "10" swaggered in its place. The day force recognized no superiors. Thus a fine competition was started, and it went on until this mill, formerly the poorest producer, was turning out more than any other mill in the plant.

The Bethlehem profit-sharing system is based on my belief that every man should get exactly what he makes himself worth. This is the only plan I know of which is equally fair to the employers and every class of employee. Someday, I hope, all labor troubles will be solved by such a system.

6

MY TWENTY THOUSAND PARTNERS

I am not a believer in large salaries. I hold that every man should be paid for personal production. Our big men at Bethlehem seldom get salaries of over one hundred dollars a week; but all of them receive bonuses—computed entirely on the efficiencies and the economies registered in their departments.

Approximately eighty per cent of the twenty-two thousand men in our plants at Bethlehem come under the operation of the system. The only ones not included are certain kinds of day laborers, whose work is of such a nature that it does not fall readily into the scheme, and the men in a few special or too-complex departments.

Take the case of a mechanic: he is given a

certain piece of work, and he knows that the allotted time for doing this work is, say, twenty hours. Perhaps he has a regular wage of forty cents an hour, irrespective of his production. If he finishes the job in the allotted twenty hours, he gets a bonus of twenty per cent., bringing his total pay for the work up to nine dollars and sixty cents. But if he does the work in twelve hours, he still receives the nine dollars and sixty cents, and is ready forthwith to tackle another piece of work. In other words, the man gets bonus pay for the job on the basis of the *entire schedule time*, regardless of the actual time it takes him to do it.

Any short cuts a man may devise or any unusual energy he may show are thus capitalized into profit for him. With this stimulus, our men are always giving their best efforts to their work, and the result has been that the production per man in some departments has more than doubled since the plan was put into effect.

We have complete schedules of time and bonus rates for many kinds of common labor, and our statistics show that such labor has been averaging nearly forty per cent above the regular rate per hour. Such jobs as wheeling a wheelbarrow or handling a shovel have been put under the profit-sharing system.

There are some departments in which the work is of such a nature that time enters very slightly into calculation—in open hearth work or treating of armor plate, for example. Here we are more concerned with the quality of the work than with the quantity turned out in a given time. In these cases we give a bonus for quality, basing our computations on tests of the steel. If we had the regular system in operation here, workmen might be tempted to hurry their work, and a lot of steel would have to be thrown out.

In still other departments we give bonuses for efficiencies. If a man handles his machines so that the item of repair is very low, or if he gets equal results with less than the regular amount of fuel, he is paid accordingly. We try to take into calculation every element that depends on the initiative, or originality, or energy, or manual dexterity of a worker.

In many departments we use $1 as a unit cost standard. The manager or superintendent gets 1 per cent, of the reduction down to $.95, 2 per cent of the total from $.95 to $.90, 3 per cent of the total from $.90 to $.85, and so on. This holds out every inducement for economy and efficiency.

We say to the superintendent of blast furnaces, for example: "This is your normal operation cost, the amount we charge up. **Everything you save from this standard cost you will share, and the more money you make the more money we will make, and the better satisfied everybody will be.**"

If Mr. Grace, the president of Bethlehem, who made a million dollars last year, were working on a salary, he would have been very well paid if he had got thirty or forty thousand dollars. But I am delighted to see him make a million. If he had made two millions the corporation would have made that much more.

We have to have a very elaborate and very costly statistical department to carry out the system, but it pays for itself a hundred times over.

There is at Bethlehem a minimum wage below which no man's salary shall fall. But most of what each worker earns is made up of bonuses. We find that if a man has not ambition enough to earn bonuses he is not likely to remain with us long.

I am very happy to know that my Bethlehem employees are the best paid body of men in the steel industry in America. Last year, from superintendents to boys, they averaged $990 apiece.

Systems of general profit sharing have certain disadvantages from which ours is free. One disadvantage is that the lazy man shares the reward of the smart man's work. General systems give employees uniformly bigger wages in times of general prosperity and furnish a good excuse to reduce wages at other times.

My system, I believe, can be fitted to any branch of industry. A banker once told me that there was no way in which it could be worked out for banks. I told him I thought there was a way. And to prove it I devised a system which has been put into successful operation in a dozen banks.

Profit sharing works well almost anywhere. I use it in my own home. Not long ago the expenses of running my New York house got exorbitant. I called in the steward and said to him: "George, I want to strike a bargain with you. I will give you ten per cent of the first thousand dollars you save in house expenses, twenty-five per cent, of the second thousand, and one-half of the third thousand."

The expense of operating the house was cut in two.

Men are pretty keen judges of their employers. **You cannot make workmen think you are interested in them unless you really are.** They realize at once whether your interest is real or assumed.

The man who gets the loyalty of his employees is the man who has, first of all, a reputation for fair dealing. Men gage fair dealing quickly and respond to it.

There has never been so much sentiment in business, so close a spirit of cooperation between employers and men, as there is today. It is time for Americans to realize the falseness of the cry that we are a nation of money-grabbers. **The difference between us and other nations is that we know how to earn money, while they, in the main, know how to save it.** The sordid, hoarding miser, who makes every sacrifice to accumulate, is so scarce with us as to cut no figure, while abroad he is everywhere.

7

MEN I HAVE
WORKED WITH

WHENEVER problems of managing men
come to my mind I think of my old master, Captain W. R. Jones, the man who, Henry
Bessemer said, knew more about steel than any
other man in America.

Old Captain Bill started in at Johnstown as
a monkey-wrench mechanic back in 1874 or
1875, and then went with Mr. Carnegie to
Braddock—Mr. Carnegie's first steel venture.
He was manager of the Braddock works when
I entered the steel business under him in 1880,
and I have never felt a deeper and more lasting
affection for any man than I had for old Captain
Bill.

Uneducated, unpolished, outspoken, old
Captain Bill was one of the most magnificent
leaders of men America has ever produced.
Everybody who worked for him idolized him,

and this idolatry made it possible for him to break all previous records in steel production.

Captain Bill could never understand the chemistry of the steel business, which was just then beginning to reform the old hit or miss program. I remember very well the first time the Pennsylvania Railroad specified that the rails we furnished should be of a certain chemical composition. This alarmed the old captain. He had never heard such names as carbon and manganese.

"Charlie," he said to me one day, "this chemistry is going to ruin the steel business yet."

In those days, of course, the steel business was in its infancy. Our expansion since then has passed belief. In 1880 the whole country produced less than a million tons of steel. In 1890 the amount had risen to five million tons; in 1900 about thirteen millions; in 1910 over twenty millions; and this year we shall produce over forty million tons of steel in America.

Once I wrote to Mr. Carnegie about a rail mill which we had designed at Braddock, and announced enthusiastically that when the mill was completed it would roll over a thousand tons of rails a day.

"I see no objection to the amount of money you want to spend," Mr. Carnegie wrote back, "but I want to exact one promise from you, that you will never tell any one we were foolish enough to suppose that this country would ever require a mill to make one thousand tons of rails a day."

Now, think of us, after this short time, making from twelve thousand to fifteen thousand tons of steel rails a day!

In 1886 it fell to my lot to roll the first steel girder that ever went into a skyscraper. At that time the business promised little. But today more than five million tons of steel are used annually for buildings. In 1901 I built the first steel railway car; now more than five million tons of steel a year are used for that purpose.

Old Captain Bill Jones was a man of many original notions. For instance, he would never take the partnership that Mr. Carnegie offered him repeatedly. He said he didn't want the men to think he was sharing the profits of the company. After trying in vain to change his manager's mind, Mr. Carnegie declared that he would always pay Captain Bill as much as the President of the United States was getting. And he always did.

The captain, I remember, used to characterize Mr. Carnegie as a wasp that came buzzing around to stir up everybody. One hot day in early summer, Mr. Carnegie sought out Jones in the works.

"Captain," he said, "I'm awfully sorry to leave you in the midst of hot metals here, but I must go to Europe. I can't stand the sultry summer in this country. You have no idea, Captain, when I get on the ship and get out of sight of land, what a relief it is to me."

"No, Andy," flashed the captain, "and you have no idea what a relief it is to me, either."

On one occasion I was talking with Herbert Spencer, Mr. Gladstone, and Mr. Carnegie in England. Each of us was supposed to contribute something entertaining to the conversation, and for a while I was rather puzzled to know what to say that would interest these famous men. Finally, I decided I would tell them some stories about the old captain, and I told them many. One of the things I prize most is a letter from Mr. Spencer recalling those stories.

While my mind is running back over those first days of the steel business, I think of William Borntrager, who did much for rolling mill development. While on a vacation William fell in love with a handsome, rather stout German girl. When he came back he told Mr. Carnegie that he wanted another vacation, so that he could get married.

Mr. Carnegie was delighted. "Tell me about the fortunate lady," he asked, "is she tall and slender and willowy?"

"Well, no, Mr. Carnegie," replied Borntrager. "Indeed, if I had had the rolling of her, I think I would have given her a few more passes."

Mr. Carnegie was the first big American business man to inaugurate a real profit-sharing system. He was the epitomization of unselfishness. **Perhaps the way in which Mr. Carnegie differed from many employers could be illustrated by calling up the picture of two boys about to feast. One says: "I have a nice pie. Come and watch me eat it." The other says: "I have a nice pie. Come, let's eat it."**

Mr. Carnegie's personality would enthuse anybody who worked for him. He had the broad views of a really big man. He was not bothered with the finicky little things that trouble so many people. When he made me manager, Mr. Carnegie said:

"Now, boy, you will see a good many things which you mustn't notice. Don't blame your men for trivial faults. If you do you will dishearten them."

When I want to find fault with my men I say nothing when I go through their departments. If I were satisfied I would praise them. My silence hurts them more than anything else in the world, and it doesn't give offense. It makes them think and work harder.

Many men fail because they do not see the importance of being kind and courteous to the men under them. Kindness to everybody always pays for itself. And, besides, it is a pleasure to be kind. I have seen men lose important positions, or their reputations—which are more important than any position—by little careless discourtesies to men whom they did not think it was worth while to be kind to.

8

WOMAN'S PART IN MAN'S SUCCESS

THERE are a good many things to be considered in selecting men for important positions. One of the things that I always take into account is their family relations. **If a man's wife takes the part of a discreet helper, or co-director with him, he is that much the more valuable to us.**

It is a common enough saying that it is harder to save money than to earn it. The women of the United States have more to learn about their husbands' money than the men have to learn about getting it. That is, men are getting more out of their earning capacities than their wives are getting out of managing the money which their husbands provide them.

I can never express the wonderful help Mrs. Schwab has been to me from the very start. Not long ago a group of men offered me a large sum, sixty million dollars, I believe, for half of Bethlehem. I told my wife about it that evening.

"This is a big sum," I said. "Half of what I have is yours. What shall we do? If we sell, your share, invested at five per cent., will bring you an income of over a hundred thousand dollars a month for the rest of your life."

"We wouldn't sell for five times that," my wife said. "What would I do with the money? And what would you do without your work?"

I have seen more men fail in business through the attitude taken by their wives in their younger days than from all the vices put together. A nagging wife, or one who is not in sympathy with a man's work, who expects impossible things of him, and is incapable of taking a general intelligent interest in his work, is one of the worst handicaps he could have. If a man works with his mind clogged by domestic troubles he is of no use to himself, his employer, or the world at large.

I don't suppose that a wife, ordinarily, should try to tell a man how to conduct his business; but she should be interested in it, and it will pay him to keep her educated about it.

I believe in people marrying young, for a happy married life is one of the best inspirations a man can have.

The question of recreation is being considered more in modern business than ever before. All men need periods of relaxation, changes of environment, mental rest. I never care how long a vacation any of my managers takes, provided that he has his end of the business up to the general level at the time he leaves, and so energized and systematized that it will stay there while he is away.

Travel broadens a man, if he keeps his eyes open. And he is sure to see many things which will help him in business. In Europe, several years ago, I went through some steel plants in Austria. Later I was talking with Emperor Francis Joseph.

"What can you find in our small and comparatively unproductive establishments to interest you?" asked the emperor, "when you have such large, splendid steel plants in America?"

"At least, Your Majesty," I replied, "I can see what to avoid."

Some of those nations across the Atlantic

have very definite divisions of aristocracy. Men in whose veins flows titled blood are vested with the right to sit in high places. **I have always believed that the aristocracy of any country should be the men who have succeeded—the men who have aided in upbuilding their country—the men who have contributed to the efficiency and happiness of their fellow men.** If America is to have an aristocracy, let it be so builded. And our future will be safe.

RECOMMENDED READING
The Classics

Wisdom of Andrew Carnegie As Told To Napoleon Hill

Napoleon Hill's Keys Positive Thinking

Magic Ladder of Success by Napoleon Hill

The Success System That Never Fails
by W. Clement Stone

Believe and Achieve by W. Clement Stone

Success Through A Positive Mental Attitude
by W. Clement Stone

Your Greatest Power by J. Martin Kohe

How To Win Friends And Influence People
by Dale Carnegie

Power of Positive Thinking by Norman Vincent Peale

Go Getter by Peter B. Kyne

I Dare You by William Danforth

University of Success by Og Mandino

Greatest Salesman in the World by Og Mandino

The Richest Man in Babylon by George Clason

Secret of Success by R.C. Allen

As A Man Thinketh by James Allen

Acres of Diamonds by Russell Conwell

Message To Garcia by Elbert Hubbard

Advantages of Poverty by Andrew Carnegie

You And Your Network by Fred Smith

See You At The Top by Zig Ziglar

Life Is Tremendous by Charlie "T" Jones

Maxims of Life & Business by John Wanamaker